AF270581

MY FRIEND WITH EPILEPSY

by Elizabeth Andrews

Cody Koala

An Imprint of Pop!
popbooksonline.com

Hello! My name is Cody Koala

This book is filled with videos, puzzles, games, and more! Scan the QR codes* while you read, or visit the website below to make this book pop.

popbooksonline.com/epilepsy

*Scanning QR codes requires a web-enabled smart device with a QR code reader app and a camera.

abdobooks.com

Published by Pop!, a division of ABDO, PO Box 398166, Minneapolis, Minnesota 55439. Copyright ©2024 by Abdo Consulting Group, Inc. International copyrights reserved in all countries. No part of this book may be reproduced in any form without written permission from the publisher. Cody Koala™ is a trademark and logo of Pop!.

Printed in the United States of America, North Mankato, Minnesota.

102023
012024

THIS BOOK CONTAINS RECYCLED MATERIALS

Cover Photo: Shutterstock Images
Interior Photos: Shutterstock Images; Getty Images
Editor: Grace Hansen
Series Designer: Victoria Bates

Library of Congress Control Number: 2023938822

Publisher's Cataloging-in-Publication Data
Names: Andrews, Elizabeth, author.
Title: My friend with epilepsy / by Elizabeth Andrews
Description: Minneapolis, Minnesota : Pop!, 2024 | Series: My friend with health needs | Includes online resources and index
Identifiers: ISBN 9781098245320 (lib. bdg.) | ISBN 9781098245887 (ebook)
Subjects: LCSH: Friendship--Juvenile literature. | Epilepsy--Juvenile literature. | Epilepsy in children--Juvenile literature. | Social acceptance--Juvenile literature.
Classification: DDC 616.853--dc23

Table of Contents

Chapter 1
Morning Medicine 4

Chapter 2
What Is Epilepsy? 8

Chapter 3
Caring for Epilepsy 12

Chapter 4
Epilepsy at School 18

Making Connections 22
Glossary 23
Index 24
Online Resources 24

Morning Medicine

It is about time for Erik to catch the school bus. His dad brings him a pill and a glass of water. Erik takes his **antiepileptic** medicine and heads out the door.

Watch a video here!

Erik has epilepsy. He's
been taking medicine to
help it for two years. He had
to go to a lot of doctors'
appointments. He took
different tests to learn he
had epilepsy.

What Is Epilepsy?

Epilepsy is a brain condition that causes **seizures**. Seizures can look different. But they all happen due to abnormal brain activity.

A person has epilepsy if they have two or more seizures with no known cause.

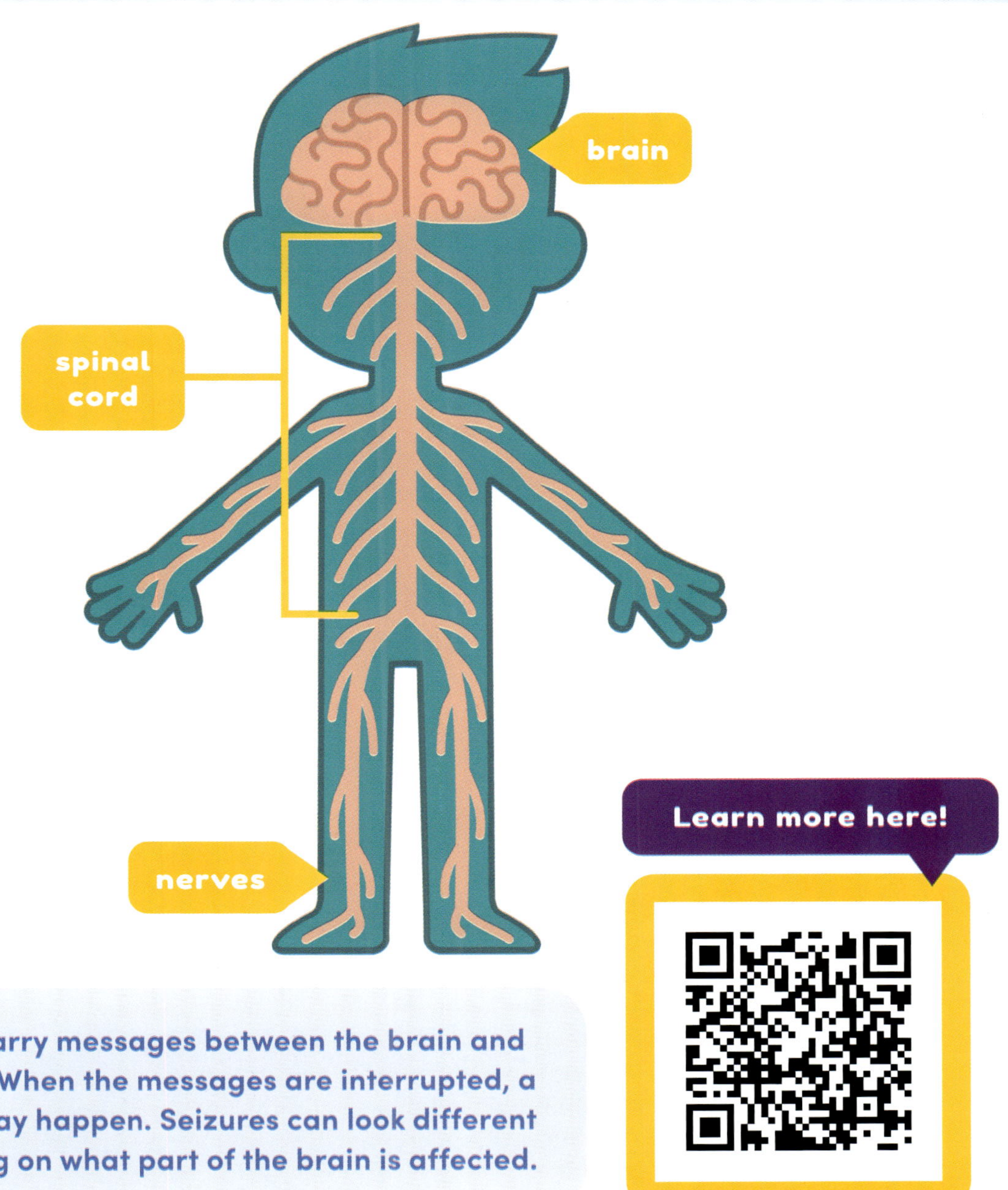

Nerves carry messages between the brain and the body. When the messages are interrupted, a seizure may happen. Seizures can look different depending on what part of the brain is affected.

Seizures can
happen when a
person is asleep.

Some seizures cause a person to look like they are staring off into space. Other seizures can cause a person to **collapse**, stiffen, and shake. People usually don't remember their seizures.

Chapter 3

Caring for Epilepsy

The most common way to care for epilepsy is with medicine. After a person is **diagnosed**, their doctor will choose the medicine most likely to stop the **seizures**.

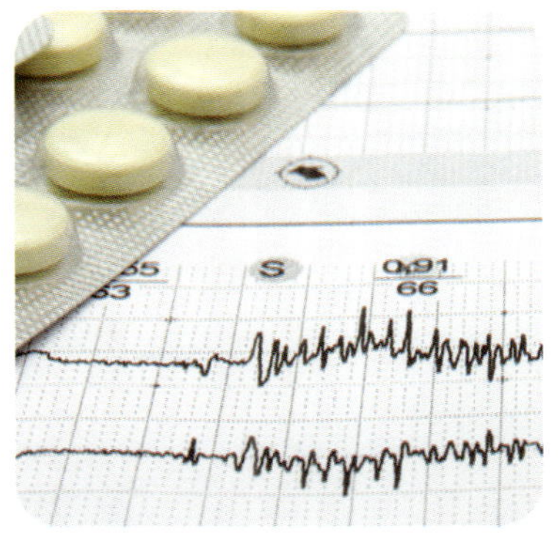

Explore links here!

Those caring for children with epilepsy take notes about what the seizures look like and how often they happen. Caregivers continue to take notes as the child starts using their medicine.

People with epilepsy may have to try different medicines to find one that works best. Some people change their **diets** to help with the condition. Others might need **surgery**.

If a person's seizures are only happening in one part of the brain, surgery may be an option to fix it.

Epilepsy at School

Caregivers, doctors, teachers, and school staff build a plan to keep students with epilepsy safe at school. If a student has a **seizure** at school, staff follow the plan to care for the student.

Complete an
activity here!

Sometimes students with epilepsy learn at a different rate than their classmates. But there are many ways to **adapt** to the condition. Children with epilepsy can be just as happy and healthy as their peers.

Making Connections

Text-to-Self

Do you or any of your friends have epilepsy? What is having epilepsy like for you or them?

Text-to-Text

Have you read any other books about people with health needs? How were those needs similar to or different from epilepsy?

Text-to-World

Many successful people have epilepsy. With the help of an adult, look up one or two people with epilepsy who interest you. Write about a few things they accomplished while having the condition.

Glossary

adapt – to become used to.

antiepileptic – especially of a medicine, used to control or prevent seizures that come with epilepsy.

collapse – to suddenly lose strength and fall down.

diagnose – to recognize something, such as a disease, by signs, symptoms, or tests.

diet – the food that a person normally eats.

seizure – an episode of interrupted brain activity that causes changes in attention and behavior.

surgery – the treating of sickness or injury by cutting into and repairing body parts.

Index

brain, 8

caregiver, 15, 18

diet, 16

doctor, 7, 12, 18

medicine, 4, 7, 12, 15–16

plan, 18

school, 4, 18, 21

seizures, 8, 11, 12, 15, 18

surgery, 16

tests, 7

Online Resources

popbooksonline.com

Thanks for reading this Cody Koala book!

This book is filled with videos, puzzles, games, and more! Scan the QR codes* while you read, or visit the website below to make this book pop.

popbooksonline.com/epilepsy

*Scanning QR codes requires a web-enabled smart device with a QR code reader app and a camera.